Martin writes with clarity on the roots of Anglican Doctrine, giving us a timely reminder of our biblical foundations and reformed heritage. I warmly commend this book to anyone who wants to engage with what it means to be Anglican.

James Hughes,
Vicar of St Alkmund's, Duffield

Deep Roots
A Beginner's Guide to the Doctrine of the Church of England

Martin Davie

The Latimer Trust

Deep Roots: A Beginner's Guide to the Doctrine of the Church of England © Martin Davie 2023. All rights reserved. ISBN 978-1-916834-00-2 Published by the Latimer Trust December 2023.

The Latimer Trust (formerly Latimer House, Oxford) is a conservative Evangelical research organisation within the Church of England, whose main aim is to promote the history and theology of Anglicanism as understood by those in the Reformed tradition. Interested readers are welcome to consult its website for further details of its many activities.

The Latimer Trust
London N14 4PS UK
Registered Charity: 1084337
Company Number: 4104465
www.latimertrust.org
administrator@latimertrust.org

Views expressed in works published by The Latimer Trust are those of the authors and do not necessarily represent the official position of The Latimer Trust.

Contents Page

Foreword to the Christian Doctrine Series	1
Introduction	5
1. The Holy Scriptures	11
2. The Fathers, the Councils and the Creeds	19
3. The Thirty-Nine Articles and the Homilies	37
4. The 1662 Book of Common Prayer and the Ordinal	51
Conclusion: Deep Roots Unreached by the Frost	63

Foreword to the Christian Doctrine Series

What does the Anglican Church teach? What should Anglicans believe? The Anglican Communion has a reputation for tolerating a wide variety of different viewpoints, so much so that it is easy to forget that there is a core of teaching, or doctrine, which Anglicans are expected to teach and believe. Most of that core is shared with other Christians to a greater or lesser extent, but there is often a distinctive way in which Anglicans relate to that common heritage and adapt it for their own mission as witnesses to Jesus Christ in the world.

There are many good studies of Anglican doctrine available, and some of them give detailed accounts for the benefit of students and theologians from other churches. Unfortunately, there is relatively little material that addresses the needs and concerns of ordinary churchgoers, many of whom have only a sketchy awareness of the Church's teaching and are baffled by an academic approach and technical terminology that they find hard to understand. The aim of this series is to present the doctrine of the Anglican Church, and in particular of the Church of England, in a format that is user friendly and that does not assume any prior knowledge of the subject. It cannot be exhaustive, but it aims to be reasonably comprehensive and to give readers a clear sense of what the Anglican Church stands for.

Anglicans do not claim to be a special kind of Christians, distinguished from others by peculiar beliefs that set them apart from the wider Christian world. On the contrary, Anglicans claim that what we believe is 'basic

Christianity' as the late John Stott put it in a book that he wrote on the subject, or 'mere Christianity' as C. S. Lewis described it in a similar volume. Anglicans adhere to the mainstream of Christian belief as this has been handed down through the centuries, and members of other Churches will find much in our heritage with which they can agree. That is as it should be, and we hope that where we take a different position to that of some other Christians, that we do so in a spirit of love and respect for them and their witness alongside our own.

In the course of time, Anglicans have rejected what they regard as aberrations in the teachings of some other Churches, and especially of the Roman Catholic Church, from which we separated at the time of the Reformation in the sixteenth century. We think that some of their doctrines have obscured the pure message of Christ and imposed beliefs that have no basis in the Bible, which is the supreme source of our faith. On other matters of controversy among Christians, Anglicans have either taken a moderate position that has tried to reconcile differences as much as possible, or else has remained silent, allowing Church members the freedom to have their own opinions without making them part of its essential beliefs. The booklets in this Series will deal with these questions and explain why Anglicans think the way they do, without condemning or dismissing the views of those who differ from us on questions where views other than our own can be defended from the Holy Scriptures that we share in common.

The aim of this Series is to guide readers through the various aspects of the Church's doctrine, avoiding technical terms as much as possible, and explaining them clearly when that is necessary. Readers who want to pursue particular subjects further are provided with a list of publications that will help them deepen their knowledge and understanding.

It is the hope of the Latimer Trust that this Series will awaken an interest among Church members in Christian beliefs that will stimulate their minds and help them grow in their faith. The Series aims to lay a foundation for the vital task of explaining what Anglicans teach and believe in a way that can be communicated positively and accurately to the wider world. It is our hope that preachers and pastors will find in it a clear presentation of the message of Jesus Christ that will guide them in their ministerial task as they proclaim the Good News of salvation to their people. May God bless them as they labour for him, and may he use the tools this Series provides for his glory and for the upbuilding of his Church.

Gerald Bray

Series Editor

Introduction

When we talk about 'the doctrine of the Church of England,' what we mean is the understanding of the apostolic teaching that is held by the Church of England. If we ask where we can find this understanding, the answer is given in Canons A5 and C15 of the Church of England's code of Canon Law, the basic set of regulations which govern the life of the Church of England, which are there in order to provide the church with good order (and therefore to promote gospel ministry and build churches).[1]

Canon A5 declares:

> The doctrine of the Church of England is grounded in the Holy Scriptures, and in such teaching of the ancient Fathers and Councils of the Church as are agreeable to the said Scriptures.
>
> In particular such doctrine is to be found in the Thirty-nine Articles of Religion, *The Book of Common Prayer*, and the Ordinal.

Canon C15 states that the Church of England:

> ...professes the faith uniquely revealed in the Holy Scriptures and set forth in the catholic creeds, which faith the Church is called upon to proclaim afresh in each

---

[1] The Canons can be found at https://www.churchofengland.org/about/leadership-and-governance/legal-services/canons-church-england/canons-website-edition or in print form as *The Canons of the Church of England*, 8th edition (London: Church House Publishing, 2022).

generation. Led by the Holy Spirit, it has born witness to Christian truth in its historic formularies, the Thirty-nine Articles of Religion, *The Book of Common Prayer* and the Ordering of Bishops, Priests and Deacons.

These two Canons give a threefold answer to the question of where the doctrine of the Church of England can be found. They tell us that if we want to know how the Church of England understands the apostolic teaching, we need to consult three authorities:

- the Holy Scriptures
- the teachings produced in the early centuries of the church's existence by the Fathers and Councils of the church and summarised in the catholic creeds
- the Church of England's three 'historic formularies' (the *Thirty-Nine Articles*, the *Book of Common Prayer* and the *Ordinal* – 'the Ordering of Bishops, Priests and Deacons')

It is important to note, however, that if we look carefully at what is said in these Canons, we find that these three authorities do not possess the same level of authority as each other. The primary authority is the Holy Scriptures, in which the apostolic faith is 'uniquely revealed,' the secondary authority is the teaching of the Fathers, the Councils and the creeds which is based on the teaching of Scripture, and the tertiary authority is the witness of the historic formularies which is based on the teaching of Scripture and of the Fathers, the Councils and the creeds.

The affirmations made by ministers of the Church of England

Those who are authorised to exercise ordained or lay ministry in the Church of England have to declare their commitment to the understanding of the apostolic teaching found in these three authorities (described as 'this inheritance of faith').

They are asked to affirm:

> ...your loyalty to this inheritance of faith as your inspiration and guidance under God in bringing the grace and truth of Christ to this generation and making Him known to those in your care.

In response they reply:

> I, A B, do so affirm, and accordingly declare my belief in the faith which is revealed in the Holy Scriptures and set forth in the catholic creeds and to which the historic formularies of the Church of England bear witness.[2]

Because they have to make this affirmation, it is necessary for ordained and lay ministers in the Church of England to have a clear grasp of the nature of the doctrinal authorities accepted by the church and what these authorities teach. Only if this is the case will they be able to keep their promise to use the teaching

---

[2] These quotations are taken from the Declaration of Assent in Canon C15 where they apply to ordained ministers. In Canons E5 and E8 they also apply to lay ministers.

contained in these authorities as their 'inspiration and guidance' in making Christ known in today's world.

It is also important that ordinary lay members of the Church of England understand what these authorities are and what they teach. This is for two reasons. First, so that they can be fed spiritually by the teaching contained in these authorities. Secondly, so that, if necessary, they will be able to challenge and correct teaching by Church of England ministers that is contrary to the doctrine which they are called to accept themselves and expound to others.

Doctrine and Law

The clergy of the Church of England are subject to its Canons, and all its members must obey parliamentary statutes and measures. These laws do not determine the Church of England's doctrine. What they do is to provide the legal framework within which Christians in the Church of England are called to live in the light of its doctrine.

In accordance with the teaching of Paul in Romans 13:1–7, members of the Church of England have a general obligation to act in obedience to the laws of the church and the state. However, if a law requires a member of the Church of England to act in a way that is contrary to the will of God as this is made known in the church's doctrine, then they would have an obligation not to obey that law based on the apostolic declaration in Acts 5:29, 'We must obey God rather than men.'

As John Stott comments:

> Christians are called to be conscientious citizens and, generally speaking, to submit to human authorities. But if the authority concerned misuses its God-given power to command what he forbids or forbid what he commands, then the Christian's duty is to disobey the human authority in order to obey God's.[3]

---

[3] John Stott, *The Message of Acts* (Leicester: InterVarsity Press, 1990), 116.

1. The Holy Scriptures

The Canons of the Church of England declare that the church's doctrine is 'grounded' in the Holy Scriptures in which the faith which the church professes is 'uniquely revealed'. What the Canons do not say is what the term 'Holy Scriptures' means. However, an explanation of its meaning is provided in Article VI of the *Thirty-Nine Articles*.

This states that, 'In the name of Holy Scripture, we do understand those Canonical books of the Old and New Testament, of whose authority was never any doubt in the Church.' The article then goes on to specify that the canonical books of the Old Testament are:

> Genesis, Exodus, Leviticus, Numbers, Deuteronomy, Joshua, Judges, Ruth, First Book of Samuel, Second Book of Samuel, First Book of Kings, Second Book of King, First Book of Chronicles, Second Book of Chronicles. First Book of Esdras, Second Book of Esdras, Book of Esther, Book of Job, Psalms, Proverbs, Ecclesiastes, or the Preacher, Cantica, or Songs of Solomon, Four Prophets the Greater, Twelve Prophets the Less.

In this list, the 'First and Second Books of Esdras' are what we would today call Ezra and Nehemiah, 'Four Prophets the Greater' are Isaiah, Jeremiah (plus Lamentations which is viewed as the work of Jeremiah), Ezekiel and Daniel, and 'Twelve Prophets the Less' are Hosea, Joel, Amos, Obadiah, Jonah, Micah, Nahum, Habakkuk, Zephaniah, Haggai, Zechariah and Malachi.

This list of the canonical books of the Old Testament is not arbitrary. By the first century there was a fixed Jewish canon of Scripture consisting of the writings now contained in the list of Old Testament books accepted by the Church of England. The New Testament tells us that Jesus accepted the books in this Jewish canon as Scripture and the Church of England is simply following his example.[1]

With reference to the New Testament, the article declares, 'All the books of the New Testament, as they are commonly received, we do receive, and account them canonical.'

The article does not say what these books are. However, from the New Testament books found in sixteenth-century English translations of the Bible and in the lectionary in the *Book of Common Prayer* and from the list of biblical books contained in the sixteenth-century code of Canon Law known as the *Reformatio Legum Ecclesiasticarum* , we know that the books concerned are the twenty-seven books that came to be accepted as canonical during the early church period, namely the four Gospels, Acts, Romans, 1 and 2 Corinthians, Galatians, Ephesians, Philippians, Colossians, 1 and 2 Thessalonians, 1 and 2 Timothy, Titus, Philemon, Hebrews, James, 1 and 2 Peter, 1, 2 and 3 John, Jude and Revelation.

As with the list of Old Testament books, this list of New Testament books is not arbitrary. It consists of those books which were either written by the apostles

---

[1] For a detailed exposition of this point see Roger Beckwith, *The Old Testament Canon of the New Testament Church* (London: SPCK, 1984).

themselves or written by those such as Luke who were associated with the apostles and who faithfully passed on their teaching. Furthermore, the message told through the books in the New Testament canon finishes the story told in the Old Testament. God's promises are kept, the Messiah comes, sin and death are defeated, and a new world is born, just as the books in the Old Testament canon say will happen.

This means that there is, in fact, one continuous canonical story which begins in the Old Testament and is finished in the New Testament. In the light of this fact, it makes perfect sense to talk not just about an Old Testament canon and a New Testament canon, but about one overarching biblical canon. Just as one can coherently say that the three parts of *The Lord of the Rings* make up one single book, so we can also coherently say that the books of the Old and New Testaments make up on single canon of Scripture, what the Christian tradition has come to call Holy Scripture or the Bible.

The authority of the canonical books

Why do the books of the Bible have doctrinal authority? There are four answers to this question.

1. The twenty-seven books of the New Testament canon contain the teaching of the apostles or of those in the circle of the apostles. It is in these books that we find the normative form of the 'the apostolic faith' or 'the faith of the Church,' the content of the teaching that was first given to the apostles by Jesus and then handed on by them to the early church. It follows that any form of teaching that seeks to teach the faith as handed down by the apostles has to be in line with what is taught in these books.

2. The New Testament books consciously build on the teaching contained in the thirty-nine books of the Old Testament, which they regard as authoritative and which they see as having been fulfilled through the saving action of God in Jesus Christ. This being the case, acceptance of the authority of the New Testament necessarily also involves acceptance of the authority of the Old Testament as well. You cannot have one without the other.

3. The writings contained in both Testaments have authority because they were inspired by God and, as such, carry God's own authority. This is something that we learn from Jesus. As John Wenham explains in his classic study, *Christ and the Bible*:

> To Christ the Bible is true, authoritative, inspired. To him the God of the Bible is the living God, and the teaching of the Bible is the teaching of the living God. To him, what Scripture says, God says.[2]

The word 'inspired' used by Wenham in this quotation explains how it can be the case that 'what Scripture says, God says.' The idea that the Bible is inspired draws on two passages from the New Testament. The first is 2 Peter 1:21 which declares that the prophetic teaching contained in Scripture is a result of the fact that 'men moved by the Holy Spirit spoke from God.' What this verse tells us is that the words of Scripture, although they are the words of human authors, are nevertheless

---

2   John Wenham, *Christ and the Bible* (Downers Grove: InterVarsity Press, 1979), 187.

the words of God, because these human authors were moved by the action of the Spirit to write as they did.

The second is 2 Timothy 3:16 which states that 'all Scripture is inspired by God.' The word translated 'inspired,' *theopneustos*, means literally 'breathed out by God' and the idea it conveys is that just as the words of human speakers are breathed out by them, so the words of Scripture are breathed out by God through the Holy Spirit.

Taken together these two verses convey the two sides of inspiration. There is a divine side, the words of Scripture being breathed out by God, and there is a human side, human authors moved by the Spirit to write these words down. Sometimes people object that 2 Peter 1:21 and 2 Timothy 3:16 only refer to the inspiration of the books of the Old Testament and that they therefore cannot be used to show the inspiration of the books of the New Testament.

However, in response to this objection it should be noted that the Spirit who was poured out on the apostles and enabled them to teach authoritatively was the same Spirit who inspired the writers of the Old Testament. This means that the same degree of inspiration can be ascribed to the apostolic writings of the New Testament as Peter and Paul ascribe to the Old Testament writings. The acceptance of the New Testament writings as forming a second biblical canon alongside the canon of the Old Testament was the church's recognition of this fact.

Two further terms used to define what is meant by inspiration are 'plenary' and 'verbal'. 'Plenary' means 'fully' and highlights the truth that all of Scripture and not just some bits of it are inspired by God and 'verbal' means that the inspiration of Scripture 'extends not just to its general message, but also to its individual words.'[3]

Like the rest of the Christian church, the Church of England has traditionally accepted the inspiration, and therefore the divine authority, of Scripture.

Thus, the homily 'An Information for them which take offence at certain places of Holy Scripture' in the Church of England's *Second Book of Homilies* states:

> For *the whole Scriptures,* saith St. Paul, *were given by the inspiration of God* (2 Timothy 3:16): and shall we Christian men think to learn the knowledge of God, and of ourselves, in any earthly man's work or writing, sooner or better than in the holy Scriptures written by the inspiration of the Holy Ghost? *The Scriptures were not brought unto us by the will of man; but holy men of God,* as witnesseth St. Peter, *spake as they were moved by the holy Spirit of God* (2 Peter 1:21).[4]

In addition, when the Church of England describes the Bible as the 'Word of God,' 'God's Word' and 'God's Word written' (Articles XVII, XIX, XX, XXI, XXII, XXIV, XXVI and XXXIV) this too reflects belief in the inspiration of Scripture. Why is Scripture 'God's Word'? Because of its plenary verbal inspiration.

---

3 Timothy Ward, *Words of Life* (Nottingham: InterVarsity Press, 2009), 87.

4 Text in Gerald Bray (ed.), *The Books of Homilies* (Cambridge: James Clarke and Co., 2015), 366.

4. The inspired words of Scripture have doctrinal authority because they tell us truthfully all that we need to know about what we should believe about God and about ourselves, and how we should act in consequence. This point is emphasised in the homily, 'A fruitful exhortation to the reading and knowledge of Holy Scripture' in the Church of England's *First Book of Homilies*. This states:

> In holy Scripture is fully contained what we ought to do, and what to eschew, what to believe, what to love, and what to look for at God's hands... in these books we shall find the Father *from* whom, the Son *by* whom, and the Holy Ghost *in* whom, all things have their being and keeping up; and these three Persons to be but one God, and one substance.
>
> In these books we may learn to know ourselves, how vile and miserable we be; and also to know God, how good he is of himself, and how he maketh us and all creatures partakers of his goodness. We may learn also in these books to know God's will and pleasure, as much as, for this present time, is convenient for us to know.[5]

For these four reasons Holy Scripture is the primary authority for the doctrine of the Church of England. It is the basis on which its doctrine is 'grounded' because

---

5   Bray (ed.), *Homilies*, 7–8.

it is the means, inspired by God and validated by Jesus himself, through which those truths we need to know in order to live rightly before God in this world and enter into God's kingdom in the next are 'uniquely revealed.'

For further reading

Roger Beckwith, *The Old Testament Canon of the New Testament Church* (London: SPCK, 1984).

Bruce Metzger, *The Canon of the New Testament* (Oxford: OUP, 1997).

Timothy Ward, *Words of Life* (Nottingham: InterVarsity Press, 2009).

John Wenham, *Christ and the Bible* (Downers Grove: InterVarsity Press, 1979).

2. The Fathers, the Councils and the Creeds

In one of his sermons, the seventeenth-century Church of England bishop Lancelot Andrewes declared:

> One canon reduced to writing by God himself, two testaments, three creeds, four general councils, five centuries, and the series of Fathers in that period – the centuries, that is, before Constantine, and two after, determine the boundary of our faith.[1]

The point that Andrewes is making is that while the primary doctrinal authority of the Church of England is the divinely inspired canon of Scripture, the boundaries of Anglican belief and practice are also determined with reference to the teaching of the Fathers, Councils and creeds of the early centuries of the church.

This is still the position of the Church of England today, and in this chapter we shall explore what we mean by the Fathers, Councils and creeds of the early church and why they should be regarded as doctrinally authoritative.

A. The Fathers

Who are the Fathers?

As we saw in chapter one, Canon A5 declares that the doctrine of the Church of England is grounded in the teaching of the 'Fathers'. The Canon itself does not say

---

[1] Lancelot Andrewes, *Opuscula Quaedam Posthuma* 91 [5], (Oxford: John Parker, 1852).

who the Fathers are, but the way the term is generally used both in the Church of England, and in the wider Christian church, tells us that the term 'Fathers' (with a capital 'F') or 'the Fathers of the church' refers to those people who have come to be recognised as the most significant teachers of the apostolic faith during the early centuries of the church (which is why the Canon refers to them as the 'ancient Fathers').[2]

As Christopher Hall explains, in the early centuries of the church, the term 'father' was in common use in both Jewish and Gentile circles as a description of a teacher of religious or philosophical truth. In line with this usage and the teaching of the New Testament itself (1 Corinthians 4:15), the apostles were referred to as Fathers, as were the bishops, and Christian teachers in general, from the second century.[3]

From the fourth century onwards, the bishops who had defended and preserved the orthodox teaching about the Trinity and the person of Christ were given the title 'father' in a more technical sense, 'as persons worthy of special regard for having preserved orthodox teaching at a time of great testing.'[4] Thus Canon 1 of the First Council of Constantinople (AD 381) refers to 'the Three

---

2 For example, this is what is meant by the Fathers in *The Early Christian Fathers* by the Church of England writer F. L. Cross (London: Duckworth, 1960) and in *The Fathers of the Church* by Pope Benedict XVI (London: Catholic Truth Society, 2008).
3 Christopher Hall, *Reading Scripture with the Church Fathers* (Downers Grove: InterVarsity Press, 1998), 49–50.
4 Hall, *Reading Scripture*, 50.

Hundred and Eighteen Fathers' assembled at Nicaea in 325.[5]

The designation 'father' also came to be given to Christian writers who were not bishops, but who were seen as having made a major contribution to teaching and defending the apostolic faith. 'Augustine, for example, calls Jerome a father even though he was not a bishop because Jerome had faithfully protected the doctrine of original sin.'[6]

Down the centuries there are four criteria that have come to be used to determine whether someone should be counted as a Father of the church.

1. Antiquity: As previously noted, a Father is someone from the early centuries of the history of the church. There is disagreement about whether the period of the Fathers should be reckoned to end in the fifth century (as Andrewes, for instance, held) or in the seventh or eighth centuries, but the title Father is not generally given to Christian teachers from later than the eighth century.

2. Holiness of life: Understood in the sense of great zeal for God and for the Scriptures. As Hall notes, at times, the Fathers:

   > ...were impatient, short-tempered, and narrow. Some had a very hard time listening to perspectives other than those they endorsed. Yet their hearts were set on fire by the

---

5 Text in *The Nicene and Post Nicene Fathers*, 2nd series, vol. XV (Edinburgh and Grand Rapids, T&T Clark/Eerdmans, 1997), 172.

6 Hall, *Reading Scripture*, 50.

> gospel. They lived and breathed the Scriptures. And many willingly laid down their lives for the sake of Christ.[7]

3. Orthodox teaching: To count as a Father, someone had to leave a legacy of teaching and that teaching had to be in line with the apostolic faith as set forth in Scripture.

4. Ecclesiastical approval: To quote Boniface Ramsey:

> This quite simply means that a Father is considered to be such by the Church at large. The most obvious sign of this approval is the designation 'saint' which is attributed to a large number of the Fathers.[8]

Today, reference is sometimes made to the so-called 'Mothers of the church'. This usage draws attention to the fact that women played a vital role in the life of the early church and that there were women such as Macrina, the sister and teacher of Basil of Caesarea and Gregory of Nyssa, who were teachers of the faith in their own right. However, the fact remains that the major public leaders and teachers of the early church were men and the traditional reference to the 'Fathers' reflects this fact.[9]

---

7   Hall, *Reading Scripture*, 51–52.
8   Boniface Ramsey, *Beginning to Read the Fathers* (London: SCM, 1993), 7.
9   For a helpful discussion of this issue see Hall, *Reading Scripture*, 43–49.

The authority of the Fathers

Unlike the writers of Scripture, the Fathers were not directly inspired by the Holy Spirit. As the Fathers themselves were the first to admit, their words were the words of human beings rather than the Word of God and as such they were capable of error and open to correction. As Augustine puts it in Letter 148 to Fortunatius:

> For the reasonings of any men whatsoever, even though they be Catholics, and of high reputation, are not to be treated by us in the same way as the canonical Scriptures are treated. We are at liberty, without doing any violence to the respect which these men deserve, to condemn and reject anything in their writings, if perchance we shall find that they have entertained opinions differing from that which others or we ourselves have, by the divine help, discovered to be the truth. I deal thus with the writings of others, and I wish my intelligent readers to deal thus with mine.[10]

It follows that the Fathers do not have the same authority as the Scriptures. This does not mean, however, that they have no authority. As the sixteenth-century Church of England writer John Jewel wrote,

---

[10] Augustine, Epistle CXLVIII in *The Nicene and Post Nicene Fathers*, First Series vol. 1 (Edinburgh and Grand Rapids: T&T Clark/Eerdmans, 1994), 502.

'They be interpreters of the Word of God.'[11] Because they are only interpreters, their authority is secondary rather than primary, but what they taught has been, and continues to be, of great importance for subsequent generations or Christian believers.

One way of understanding this is to say that the while the Scriptures are the foundation of Christian doctrine, by their interpretation of the Scriptures the Fathers erected a solid doctrinal structure on this foundation and what subsequent generations of Christians have done is develop or extend this structure. Another way of making the same point is to say that the Fathers began a helpful conversation about how to understand the Scriptures rightly – and what subsequent generations of Christians have done is continue this conversation.

The key things we learn from the Fathers

The reason why subsequent generations of Christians have developed and extended the doctrinal structure erected by the Fathers is because they have recognised that the Fathers taught and defended key elements of the apostolic faith that could otherwise have been forgotten or set aside. These key elements are as follows:

1. Scripture is God's inspired word and, as such, the supreme authority for Christian belief and conduct; the key calling of Christian ministers is to teach and preach it.
2. There is one all good and all wise God who has created and sustains all things that exist.

---

[11] John Ayre (ed.), *The Works of John Jewel, The Fourth Portion* (Cambridge: CUP, 1850), 1173.

3. This one God exists as a Trinity of three Persons, God the Father, God the Son and God the Holy Spirit, who are all, in every respect, equally God.

4. God created human beings, who are male and female and who consist of a physical body and a non-corporeal soul, as good creatures. However, at the instigation of the devil, the first ancestors of the human race rebelled against God. As a result, all subsequent human beings have a fallen nature which makes them sinners who are incapable of living in obedience to God, which means that they are subject to physical and spiritual death.

5. In order to change this situation, God the Son, while remaining God, took human nature upon himself in the womb of the virgin Mary. As Jesus Christ, he died and rose again in order to be a sacrifice that assuaged the wrath of God against human sin and that overcame the power of the devil over the human race. His sacrifice made it possible for human beings to be regarded as righteous before God and to be resurrected to enjoy eternal life in his presence.

6. People receive the benefit of what Christ has done when, as a result of the grace of God, they believe and are baptised. Good works done apart from faith are spiritually unfruitful, but good works will necessarily be the result of genuine faith.

7. At the end of time, Christ will return in glory and will judge the living and the dead. The faithful will be admitted into God's eternal kingdom, but the wicked will be consigned to eternal damnation.

8. At Baptism, those who are baptised receive the forgiveness of sins and the gift of the Holy Spirit. They receive adoption as God's children and are renewed as God's image. It is legitimate

for infants as well as adults to be baptised, and those who are baptised should also subsequently receive prayer from a bishop for the sevenfold gifts of the Spirit listed in Isaiah 11:2, this prayer being accompanied by the laying on of hands and/or anointing with the oil of chrism.

9. At Holy Communion, the faithful are spiritually strengthened by receiving the body and blood of Christ. The bread and wine remain bread and wine, but those who receive them with faith partake spiritually of the body of Christ which was broken for them and the blood of Christ which was shed for them.

10. God has established through the apostles a threefold pattern of ordained ministry consisting of bishops, presbyters and deacons. The role of deacons is to assist the bishops and presbyters and the main roles of bishops and presbyters are to preach and teach, administer Baptism and the Eucharist, provide pastoral care, and exercise pastoral discipline (the 'power of the keys'). Bishops alone have the right to ordain.

B. The Councils

Which are the Councils referred to in Canon A5?

Just as Canon A5 does not tell us who the Fathers are, so likewise it does not tell us which 'Councils' it has in mind. However, the Canon's use of the term 'ancient' to refer to the Councils as well as to the Fathers tells us that it is referring to councils from the early centuries of the church.

There were a large number of church councils held in this period, but in the subsequent history of the church there are six which have been held in particular regard both by the church in general and by the Church of England (this regard often being indicated by referring to them as Councils with a capital 'C'). The homily 'On the Peril of Idolatry' in the Church of England's *Second Book of Homilies* refers, for example, to the 'six Councils which were allowed and received of all men.'[12] These six Councils, which were primarily Councils of bishops, are:

1. The First Council of Nicaea (325)
5. The First Council of Constantinople (381)
6. The First Council of Ephesus (431)
7. The Council of Chalcedon (451)
8. The Second Council of Constantinople (553)
9. The Third Council of Constantinople (680)

These Councils are referred to as 'general' Councils because they were Councils of the whole church rather than of particular churches, or groups of churches, and they are also referred to as 'ecumenical' Councils because they were attended by bishops from across the Roman world.

The authority of the Councils

The Church of England is clear that, like the Fathers, but unlike Scripture, councils of the church are not to be regarded as infallible. Article XXI declares that even

---

12 Bray (ed.), *Homilies*, 240.

'General Councils ... may err, and sometimes have erred, even in things pertaining unto God.'

The six councils listed above have, nonetheless, traditionally been seen as having a secondary doctrinal authority. This is because these councils upheld key elements of the apostolic faith at a time when heretical forms of teaching threatened to undermine them.

1. The First Council of Nicaea upheld the truth that God the Son possesses exactly the same divine nature as God the Father (saying that he is *homoousios*, of the same nature, as the Father).

10. The First Council of Constantinople reiterated the truth of the divine nature of God the Son upheld at Nicaea, and also upheld the truth that the Holy Spirit likewise fully possesses the same divine nature possessed by the Father and the Son.

11. The First Council of Ephesus upheld the truths that Jesus Christ is one person rather than two, God the Son and the human Jesus of Nazareth, and that the result of original sin is that human beings cannot attain salvation solely through the exercise of their own free will, but only through the supernatural grace of God.

12. The Council of Chalcedon upheld the truths already upheld at Nicaea, Constantinople and Ephesus and further upheld the truth that Christ is one person who has both a divine nature and a human nature.

13. The Second Council of Constantinople upheld the truths taught by the four previous councils.

14. The Third Council of Constantinople upheld the truths taught by the first four councils and in

addition upheld the truth that because Christ has both a divine and a human nature, he therefore has both a divine and a human will.

In upholding these truths these councils give a faithful interpretation of the apostolic faith as taught in the Scriptures. For this reason, the teaching of these councils provides a reliable basis for the teaching of the Church of England today. To put the same point the other way round, if those in the Church of England are not teaching the truths upheld by these councils then this is a clear indication that their teaching has departed from the apostolic faith and needs to be corrected.

C. The catholic creeds

Canon C15 refers to the 'catholic creeds' which Article VIII of the *Thirty-Nine Articles* defines as the Nicene Creed, the Athanasian Creed and the Apostles' Creed. They are called the 'catholic' creeds because they express the faith held by the church in general (the catholic or universal church) rather than simply by particular churches.

The Nicene Creed

The Nicene Creed is a fourth-century creed, which was originally written in Greek. It is called the Nicene Creed because it embodies the belief in the divinity of God the Son upheld by the First Council of Nicaea in 325. It seems to have been composed at (or shortly after) the First Council of Constantinople in 381 which re-affirmed the Nicene faith, and it was officially recognised as summarising the theology of that Council at Chalcedon in 451.[13] Because of its association with the First Council of Constantinople, it is sometimes referred to as the Niceno-Constantinopolitan Creed.

Following the Council of Chalcedon, this creed came to be viewed as a touchstone of Christian orthodoxy in both the Eastern and Western church and from the sixth century onwards it became the creed recited in the liturgy. At the Reformation, it was retained by the Church of England as the creed to be said at Holy Communion and it continues to be used in the church to this day.

Following a pattern that goes back at least as far as the second century, the Nicene Creed is divided into three parts which declare belief in God as Father, Son and Holy Spirit.

The first part declares belief that God the Father is the creator of all that exists, whether this is material ('visible') or spiritual ('invisible'). This does not mean that the Son and the Holy Spirit are not involved in God's creative activity, but rather that the pattern of God's activity is that God the Father creates through the activity of the Son and the Spirit.

The second part declares belief that the Son was not created by the Father but comes forth from the being of the Father (which is what 'begotten' means) and therefore shares the Father's divine nature (which is what 'God of God, Light of Light, Very God of Very God' and 'of one being with the Father' mean). It also declares belief in the fact that in order to save the human

---

13 See J. N. D. Kelly, *Early Christian Creeds*, 3rd edition (London: Longman, 1972), chapters VIII–XI.

race, the Son became incarnate, died, was buried, rose, ascended and will come again in judgement.

The third part declares belief that the Spirit proceeds from the Father and the Son. He therefore shares their divine nature. That is why he can give life at creation and new life in salvation and why he is rightly 'worshipped and glorified' alongside the Father and the Son. It also declares that the Spirit inspired the Old Testament's prophetic witness to Christ and that the Spirit's work bears fruit in the existence of the church, the forgiveness of sins at Baptism, and will bear fruit in the resurrection of the dead at the end of time and the life in the world to come that will result from that.

The original form of the Nicene Creed simply said that the Spirit 'proceeds from the Father' (John 15:26). The words 'and the Son' were then added by the Western church to reflect the biblical witness that although the Spirit proceeds from the Father, he also comes from the Son.

The Athanasian Creed

The Athanasian Creed is a Western creed that was originally written in Latin in the area of Lérins in what is now Southern France, at the end of the fifth or the beginning of the sixth century. Calling it the Creed of Athanasius, who had been persecuted for his orthodox beliefs, was a way of saying: 'This is the faith to which Athanasius remained loyal and for which he was prepared to suffer. You should be prepared to follow his example by remaining equally loyal to it.'

This creed is also known as the *Quicunque vult* (English 'whoever wishes') which are its opening words in

Latin. Although it was probably written as a teaching tool rather than for liturgical use, it came to be used in the liturgy across the Western church (including the Church in England) from the eighth century onwards. Its use was continued in the Church of England at the Reformation and today it is authorised for use at both Morning Prayer and Holy Communion.

The creed begins and ends with what are known as the 'damnatory clauses' so called because they declare that belief in the catholic (worldwide or universal) faith is necessary to avoid damnation. The rest of the creed is divided into two sections, the first concerned with the Trinity and the second with person and work of Christ. In between are two verses that serve as a hinge holding the two main sections together and further emphasising the importance of right belief for salvation.

On the Trinity, the creed teaches that there is one God who exists as three Persons, the Father, the Son and the Holy Spirit. Because they are all God, all three Persons possess the same divine attributes (thus they are all 'uncreated,' 'infinite' and 'eternal' and they possess the same divine names, 'Almighty,' 'God' and 'Lord').

What distinguishes the Persons is their relationships of origin, the Father being neither created nor begotten, the Son being not created but begotten from the Father, and the Spirit being neither created nor begotten, but proceeding from the Father and the Son.

On the person and work of Christ, the creed teaches that Christ is 'perfect God and perfect Man' – one person with both a divine and human nature. It also teaches that as the God–Man he died, descended to the place of the dead, rose, ascended and will come to judge the living and the dead.[14]

The damnatory clauses in the creed are a stumbling block to many who accept the rest of its teaching. However, they make sense once one understands that according to the New Testament salvation involves faith in Christ (see Mark 16:16, John 3:16–18, Romans 3:28). Faith in Christ, in turn, means faith in the teaching of the apostles who are the ambassadors appointed by Christ to speak on his behalf (2 Corinthians 5:20) and, by extension, faith in later church teaching ('the catholic faith') which embodies the teaching of the apostles. Accordingly, to turn away from the catholic faith is, as the creed says, to exclude oneself from salvation by rejecting faith in Christ himself.

The Apostles' Creed

The Apostles' Creed is so called because of a legend which says it was composed by the apostles themselves under the direct inspiration of the Holy Spirit on the day of Pentecost. However, in reality, it is a development of what is known by scholars as the Old Roman Creed, a confession of faith which seems to have been originally written in Greek and which can be traced back to the middle of the second century. The present form of the creed, originally written in Latin, may have originated in what is now south-west France

---

14   This is what is meant in older translations of the Athanasian and Apostles' Creeds when they say that Christ 'descended into hell.' Following his death Christ went as a disembodied spirit to the place of the dead (the old English word for which was 'hell') until the time of this resurrection. Support for Christ's descent to the place of the dead can be found in Luke 23:43, Acts 2:4–31, 1 Peter 3:19–20 and 4:6.

sometime in the seventh century. Under the influence of the Emperor Charlemagne, it came to be used in the Western church (including the Church in England) as the standard statement of basic Christian belief from the ninth century onwards.[15]

The creed was retained by the Church of England at the Reformation and is used today at services of Morning and Evening Prayer, and at Baptism services. It also the creed used in the Catechism in the *Book of Common Prayer*.

Like the Nicene Creed, the Apostles' Creed is a three-part declaration of faith in the Triune God. It declares the basic tenets of the Christian faith as taught from the time of the apostles onwards, but without the added levels of doctrinal precision that we find in the other two creeds.

The first part declares faith in God the Father as the creator of heaven and earth.

The second part declares faith in Jesus, God's Son and our Lord, the person who became incarnate through the virgin birth, died, descended to the place of the dead, rose, ascended, and will return as judge of the living and the dead.

The third part declares faith in the Holy Spirit and in the church, the forgiveness of sins, the resurrection of the body and eternal life as the fruit of the Spirit's work.

---

[15] For details, see Kelly, chapters IV–V and XII–XII.

The authority of the creeds

The authority of the catholic creeds lies in the fact that they bear faithful witness to the faith taught by the apostles, passed on in written form in the New Testament, and upheld by the orthodox Fathers and Councils of the early church.

Taken together the catholic creeds declare truthfully who God is, who Jesus Christ is, what God, Father, Son and Holy Spirit has done, is doing and will do in his acts of creation and salvation, and finally the fact that we need to hold fast to these truths if we wish to be saved.

For this reason, they constitute a reliable secondary authority for the doctrine of the Church of England today.

For further reading

Henry Bettenson, *The Early Christian Fathers* (Oxford: OUP, 1969).

Henry Bettenson, *The Later Christian Fathers* (Oxford: OUP, 1973).

Martin Davie, *The Athanasian Creed* (London: Latimer Trust, 2019).

J. N. D. Kelly, *Early Christian Doctrines* (London: A&C Black, 1980).

J. N. D. Kelly, *Early Christian Creeds* (London: Longman, 1972).

3. The Thirty-Nine Articles and the Homilies

As we saw in chapter one, the third form of doctrinal authority recognised by the Church of England is that of the three 'historic formularies' – the *Thirty-Nine Articles*, the *Book of Common Prayer* and the 1662 *Ordinal*. In this chapter we shall look at the purpose and nature of these 'historic formularies' and the reason why each of them possesses tertiary doctrinal authority.

A. The Thirty-Nine Articles

The purpose of the Articles

Following the breach with Rome in the 1530s, the leaders of the Church of England felt it needed to draw up a statement of its faith and practice, 'for avoiding of diversities of opinion, and for the establishment of consent touching true religion.'

The leaders of the Church of England wanted to avoid 'diversities of opinion' because they believed that this was incompatible with maintenance of proper order in church and state, and because they believed that to allow unlimited diversity would mean tolerating error in important areas of the church's faith and practice.

What they wanted instead was 'consent touching true religion.' By 'true religion' they meant the teaching and practice of Jesus and his apostles as recorded in the New Testament, expounded by the orthodox Fathers and Councils of the church during the first few centuries of its history, and summarised in the creeds. The *Thirty-Nine Articles* were intended to help embody true religion in the life of the Church of England both by setting out a pattern for the faith and practice based on these sources and by ruling out the errors of medieval Catholicism on the one hand and of the radical Reformation on the other.

The development of the Articles

Originally there were forty-two articles, promulgated in English and Latin in 1553, but they were revised and condensed into thirty-nine ten years later. Initially, Queen Elizabeth I refused to accept Article XXIX on the Lord's Supper, but that was reinstated in 1571 when the Articles reached the form that we still have today.

All clergy were required to subscribe to them, a practice that continues to this day in the affirmations made by clergy and lay ministers when they are ordained.

The content of the Articles

The *Thirty-Nine Articles* can be divided into eight sections.

The first section begins the Articles with a set of five articles on the doctrine of God:

I	Of Faith in the Holy Trinity
II	Of Christ the Son of God
III	Of his going down into Hell
IV	Of his Resurrection
V	Of the Holy Ghost

Following the teaching of the Bible and the catholic creeds, these articles affirm that God is eternally Father, Son and Holy Spirit, that Jesus Christ is true God and true Man, that Christ became incarnate in the womb of the virgin Mary, died for our sins, descended to the dead, rose bodily from the grave and ascended bodily into heaven, and finally that the Holy Spirit who proceeds from the Father and the Son is truly and eternally God.

The second section is a set of three articles on Scripture and the creeds:

VI	Of the Sufficiency of the Scripture
VII	Of the Old Testament
VIII	Of the Three Creeds

These articles explain that 'Holy Scripture containeth all things necessary for salvation' and that Scripture means the sixty-six books of the Old and New Testaments. They also declare that the while the liturgical, political and social arrangements that we find in the Old Testament may no longer be binding, its underlying moral teaching ('the commandments called moral') still is, and that the catholic creeds are to be accepted because what they say agrees with the Bible.

The third section is a long sequence of ten articles on sin and salvation:

IX	Of Original or Birth-sin
X	Of Free-Will
XI	Of Justification

XII	Of Good Works
XIII	Of Works before Justification
XIV	Of Works of Supererogation
XV	Of Christ alone without Sin
XVI	Of Sin after Baptism
XVII	Of Predestination and Election
XVIII	Of obtaining eternal Salvation only by the Name of Christ

These articles teach that all human beings, Christ excepted, need salvation due to original and actual sin and that salvation is possible because those who believe in Christ (and they alone) are justified by faith. They say that good works are not the cause of our justification, but that they necessarily flow from it in the same way that a good tree will necessarily produce good fruit. They declare that justification by faith is the result of God's decision to elect to eternal life all who accept the promise of salvation given in Scripture, and that even serious sin committed after Baptism can be forgiven if we repent and turn back to God.

The fourth section contains three articles on the nature and authority of the church:

XIX	Of the Church
XX	Of the Authority of the Church
XXI	Of the Authority of General Councils

These articles define the visible church of God as the community of professing Christians in which Scripture is preached and the sacraments are rightly administered. They warn that the visible church is always subject to error and declare that although the church has the authority to determine rites and ceremonies and to adjudicate theological controversies, it does not have the authority to go against the teaching of Scripture. Finally, they note that General Councils of the church are also subject to error and that they cannot rightly define anything as being necessary for salvation unless this definition can be derived from Scripture.

The fifth section consists of a set of articles errors concerning various errors relating to the practice of the church:

XXII	Of Purgatory
XXIII	Of Ministering in the Congregation
XXIV	Of Speaking in the Congregation

These articles reject belief in purgatory and the church's right to issue pardons to reduce time in purgatory. They reject also the adoration of images and relics and the invocation of the saints. They lay down that it is not right for anyone to minister in the church without having received authorisation to do so from those whose role it is to give it. Finally, they declare it is wrong to conduct worship 'in a tongue not understanded of the people.'

The sixth section is a sequence of seven articles on the sacraments:

XXV	Of the Sacraments
XXVI	Of the Unworthiness of Ministers
XXVII	Of Baptism
XXVIII	Of the Lord's Supper
XXIX	Of the Wicked which eat not the Body of Christ
XXX	Of both kinds
XXXI	Of Christ's one Oblation

These articles teach that there are two sacraments, Baptism and the Lord's Supper, and that the personal unworthiness of the minister administering them does not invalidate them. They say that Baptism (which includes infant Baptism) is an efficacious sign of 'regeneration or new birth' by means of which those who receive it with faith 'are grafted into the Church; the promises of the forgiveness of sin, and of our adoption to be the sons of God, by the Holy Ghost are visibly signed and sealed; faith is confirmed, and grace increased by virtue of prayer unto God.' They further declare that at the Lord's Supper for those who 'rightly, worthily and with faith' receive them (and for them only), partaking of the bread and wine results in being spiritually fed by partaking of the body and blood of Christ.

These articles also insist that the Lord's Supper is not a fresh sacrificial offering to God of the body and blood of Christ, that the bread and wine consecrated at the Lord's Supper remain bread and wine, and that is wrong to reserve, process, elevate or worship the bread once it has been consecrated.

The seventh section contains five articles on various aspects of the church's discipline:

XXXII	Of the Marriage of Priests
XXXIII	Of Excommunicate Persons
XXXIV	Of the Traditions of the Church
XXXV	Of the Homilies
XXXVI	Of Consecrating of Ministers

These articles teach that the clergy may marry, that excommunication should be practised, that traditions and ceremonies may vary in different national churches and should be respected unless they are contrary to Scripture, that the model sermons contained in the Church of England's *First and Second Book of Homilies* contain 'godly,' 'wholesome,' and 'necessary' doctrine, and finally that the Church of England's ordination rites contain all the necessary elements for the ordination and consecration of bishops, priests and deacons while containing nothing that is 'superstitious and ungodly.'

Finally, the eighth section concludes with three articles that address different aspects of the relationship between Christians and civil society:

XXXVII	Of Civil Magistrates
XXXVIII	Of Christian Men's Goods
XXXIX	Of a Christian Man's Oath

These articles affirm and explain the role of the monarch as the supreme governor of the Church of England and deny the jurisdiction in England of the Bishop of Rome. They defend the right of the state to take life when necessary and the legitimacy of Christians serving in the military. They say that Christians must practise charity towards those in need, but that the goods of Christians do not need to be held in common, and that Christians may take oaths providing that this is done truthfully and for a legitimate reason.

The authority of the Articles

The reason why the *Thirty-Nine Articles* rightly function as a tertiary authority in the Church of England is because, in the words of J. I. Packer, they provide 'explanatory echoes of the apostolic witness to Christ.'[1]

To put it another way, the Articles have authority because they achieve what they were intended to achieve, namely to provide the basis for 'consent concerning true religion,' by setting forth a pattern for the faith and practice of the Church of England that is in accordance with the teaching and practice of Jesus and his apostles as recorded in the New Testament, expounded by the orthodox Fathers and Councils of the church during the first few centuries of its history,

---

1 J. I. Packer, *The Thirty-Nine Articles* (London: Pastoral Aid Society, 1961), 44.

and summarised in the creeds. If you compare what is taught in the Articles to what is taught in these other sources, you will find that they cohere.

Because this is the case, those in the Church of England today can turn with confidence to the Articles as a trustworthy source for their own theology and practice and for the theology and practice they teach to others.

B. The Homilies

The purpose of the Homilies

As noted above, the homilies contained in the *First and Second Books of Homilies* are model sermons. The reason that the *Homilies* were produced was because the leaders of the Tudor Church of England knew that the parochial clergy could not be relied on to preach biblical doctrine or preach it in an effective manner. The purpose of the *Homilies* was to provide that 'honest remedy' by giving pre-written material to be used by clergy who were not licensed to preach the own sermons, but who still needed to give instruction to their people.

The contents of the Homilies

The *First Book of Homilies* (which was first published in 1547) contains five types of material.

1. The opening homily, 'A Fruitful Exhortation to the Reading of Holy Scripture,' sets the tone for the whole collection by emphasising that it is through knowledge of and obedience to Scripture

that we can live in the way that God requires and so attain eternal life.

2. The homilies, 'Of the misery of all mankind,' 'Of the salvation of mankind by only Christ,' 'Of the true, lively and Christian Faith' and 'Of good works annexed unto Faith,' explain the doctrine of justification by faith and the importance of good works as an expression of saving faith.

3. The homilies, 'Of Christian Love and Charity,' 'How dangerous a thing it is to fall from God' and 'Against the Fear of Death,' warn of the nature and importance of Christian love and against apostasy and the fear of death.

4. The homily, 'Concerning Good Order and Obedience,' explains that Christians need to obey the civil authorities appointed by God.

5. The homilies, 'Against Swearing and Perjury,' 'Against Whoredom and Uncleanness' and 'Against Contention and Brawling,' warn against three forms of personal immorality.

Taken together, these homilies give an overall introduction to what it means to live a godly life, rightly responding to what God has done for us in Christ, and highlighting certain aspects of Christian conduct which were seen as needing particular emphasis.

The *Second Book of Homilies* (first published in 1563, with an additional homily being added in 1571) contains four types of material.

1. There are several homilies which supply appropriate teaching for the each of the major festivals in the Christian year so that congregations could understand what was being celebrated. This teaching can be found

in the homilies, 'Of the Nativity of Christ,' 'Of the Passion of Christ,' 'Of the Resurrection of Christ,' 'Of the Gifts of the Holy Ghost' and 'For the Rogation-days' which provide homilies for Christmas, Easter and Pentecost and for the key agricultural festival of Rogationtide.

2. There are homilies which reinforce the teaching given in the *First Book of Homilies*. The homily 'Of the reverend estimation of God's Word' reinforces the teaching of the homily 'A Fruitful Exhortation to the Reading of Holy Scripture' in the earlier collection by responding to some common objections to the biblical material such as the ungodly lifestyle of the Old Testament patriarchs or the curses against the wicked contained in the Psalms. The homily 'Of Repentance' underlines the teaching of the earlier homilies – 'Of the salvation of mankind by only Christ,' 'Of the true, lively and Christian Faith' and 'Of Good works annexed unto faith' – by explaining that reconciliation to God involves repentance, faith in the promises of salvation God concerning salvation through Christ and amendment of life resulting in the performance of good works. Finally, the 1571 homily 'Against Rebellion' underlines the teaching of the earlier homily 'Concerning Good Order and Obedience' by stressing the importance of obeying the rulers appointed by God and the unlawfulness of rebellion against them.

3. There are homilies which give guidance about the kind of behaviour that Christians should engage in and the sort of behaviour that they should avoid. These topics are covered by the homilies 'Of Good Works: first of Fasting,' 'Against Gluttony and Drunkenness,' 'Against

Excess of Apparel,' 'Of Alms-doing,' 'Of the state of Matrimony,' and 'Against Idleness'.

4. There are homilies which give guidance about the nature and importance of Christian worship and, related to this, the need to keep churches clean and in good repair. We can see this purpose reflected in the homilies 'Of the right Use of the Church,' 'Against peril of Idolatry,' 'Of the repairing and keeping clean of Churches,' 'Of Prayer,' 'Of the Place and Time of Prayer,' 'That Common Prayers and Sacraments ought to be ministered in a known tongue,' and 'Of the worthy receiving of the Sacrament of the Body and Blood of Christ.'

The importance of the Homilies today

Sadly, the Homilies are little known and very rarely used in the contemporary Church of England. However, this should not be the case. The Homilies cannot be disregarded by anyone who accepts that the *Thirty-Nine Articles* provide authoritative guidance for the contemporary church. This is for three reasons.

1. Article XI explicitly refers to the homily 'Of the salvation of mankind by only Christ' ('the Homily of Justification') as giving further explanation about why the teaching 'that we are justified by faith only' is 'a most wholesome doctrine and full of comfort.' The homily acts as the authoritative commentary on the article.

15. As Article XXXV says, the teaching contained in the two books of homilies is 'godly' because it is in accordance with the teaching given by God in Scripture. It is 'wholesome' (in other words, spiritually health giving) because it gives truthful teaching about God and how he wants people to

behave, thus enabling them to respond in faith and obedience. It is 'necessary for the times' because many of the issues it addresses are still important for Christians today.

16. On the subjects on which they overlap, the *Homilies* and the *Thirty-Nine Articles* contain the same basic teaching, with the *Homilies* giving this teaching in more detail. It is therefore not possible to play off the teaching of the articles against the teaching of the homilies. If you accept the one, you are obliged to accept the other.

For further reading

Gerald Bray, *The Faith We Confess* (London: Latimer Trust 2009). Gerald Bray (ed.), *The Books of Homilies* (Cambridge: James Clarke and Co., 2015).

Martin Davie, *Our Inheritance of Faith* (Malton: Gilead Books 2013).

Ashley Null, 'Official Tudor Homilies' in P. McCullough, H. Adlington and E. Rhatigan (eds), *The Oxford Handbook of the Early Modern Sermon* (Oxford: OUP, 2011), 348–365.

J. I. Packer and Roger Beckwith, *The Thirty-Nine Articles: Their Place and Use Today* (Oxford: Latimer Trust, 1984).

4. The 1662 Book of Common Prayer and the Ordinal

A. The Book of Common Prayer

The principles underlying the Book of Common Prayer

The principles underlying the *Book of Common Prayer* are explained in the section at the start of the book entitled 'Concerning the Service of the Church'.

This section first of all explains what the English Reformers saw as wrong with the late medieval patterns of worship that the *Book of Common Prayer* replaced. It argues that a 'godly and decent' order of worship had been developed by the Fathers, but that this had subsequently become corrupted in medieval practice:

- The biblical books were not read through in their entirety.
- Most of the Psalms were not read.
- The services were read in Latin rather than in the vernacular.
- The rules governing which parts of the service to use were very difficult to follow.

Having made these criticisms, the Preface to the Prayer Book goes on to enunciate four principles that guide it:

- It is biblically based and those things that are untrue, uncertain, vain or superstitious have been left out.

- The biblical books are to be read through continuously rather than being broken up into disconnected pieces.

- It is in a language that can be understood – in other words, in English rather than Latin (although the use of Latin was still allowed in contexts where it would be understood, such as the universities).

- The rules that govern the service are few and simple.

There is also to be one uniform liturgy for the whole country rather than a diversity of local rites. This was what was meant by the term 'common prayer'. If we ask why the English Reformers felt that a single uniform liturgy was important the answer is because (a) experience had taught that the multiplicity of medieval rites produced liturgical confusion and (b) a single uniform rite guaranteed that a reformed and godly liturgy would (in principle at least) be used across all the parishes in the country. In line with the Old Testament accounts of the reformation of the worship of Judah by godly monarchs such as Hezekiah and Josiah (2 Chronicles 29–31 and 34–35), their vision was for a united Christian country under a godly monarch in which everyone worshipped together in a proper and godly way, thus helping to ensure the unity of the country ('the country that prays together stays together') and its blessing by God.

The development of the Book of Common Prayer

The first version of the *Book of Common Prayer*, which was edited by Archbishop Cranmer and which drew on a wide range of sources going back to the Fathers, was issued in 1549. A second revised edition (again edited by Cranmer) was issued in 1552, and again in 1559 with three further changes following the accession of Elizabeth I. There were some further additions in 1604, including the Catechism.

During the sixteenth and early seventeenth centuries, the Puritan party in the Church of England argued for the Prayer Book to be further revised on the grounds that it was still too like the liturgy of the Roman Catholic Church.

In 1645, the *Book of Common Prayer* was officially abolished by Parliament. It was replaced by the *Directory for the Public Worship of God* which, unlike the *Book of Common Prayer*, did not contain detailed liturgy but was instead an outline of the necessary elements for each of the services that was to be developed by each minister as they felt appropriate.

However, in 1662, the *Book of Common Prayer* was revised once more and ratified by Parliament. With only a few minor alterations it has remained in use in the Church of England ever since.

The contents of the Book of Common Prayer

A careful study of its contents shows that the *Book of Common Prayer*, like the *Thirty-Nine Articles*, can be divided into eight sections.

1. The opening three items give the principles that determine the overall contents of the Prayer Book:

- The Preface
- Concerning the Service of the Church
- Of Ceremonies

2. Following this are the rules for using the material in the Prayer Book, including the list of which biblical readings are to be used when:

- Rules to Order the Service
- The Order how the Psalter is appointed to be read
- The Order how the rest of the Holy Scripture is appointed to be read
- A Table of Proper Lessons and Psalms
- The Calendar, with the Table of Lessons
- The Revised Tables of Lessons (1922)
- Tables and Rules for the Feasts and Fasts through the whole Year

3. Next, there is liturgical material for daily services of Morning and Evening Prayer and for the celebration of Holy Communion, together with the text of the Athanasian Creed:

- The Order for Morning Prayer
- The Order for Evening Prayer
- The Creed of St. Athanasius
- The Litany
- Prayers and Thanksgivings
- Collects, Epistles, and Gospels
- Holy Communion

4. A series of services running from the 'Public Baptism of Infants' to 'The thanksgiving of women after childbirth' covers the whole of life from the cradle to the grave. The Catechism is included in this section because it is designed to provide instruction in Christian belief and behaviour for those baptised as infants in order to prepare them for confirmation.

- Public Baptism of Infants
- Private Baptism of Children
- Baptism of those of Riper Years
- A Catechism
- The Order of Confirmation
- The Solemnization of Matrimony
- The Visitation of the Sick
- The Communion of the Sick
- The Burial of the Dead
- The Thanksgiving of Women after Child-bearing

5. The Prayer Book includes 'A Commination (Or denouncing of God's anger and judgement against sinners)' which allows for an act of corporate reflection on the seriousness of sin and the need to repent of it.

6. It also incorporates 'The Psalter' which provides a uniform English edition of the Psalms for everyone to use in public worship.

7. There are two sets of prayers for use in special circumstances:

- Forms of Prayer to be used at Sea
- Forms of Prayer for the Anniversary of the day of the Accession of the Reigning Sovereign

8. There are two final sections, which are essentially appendices: the 'Articles of Religion' (to underline the doctrinal underpinnings of the liturgy) and 'A Table of Kindred and Affinity' which lists who may not be married to whom (for example, a man may not marry his mother or daughter, or a woman her father or son).

The authority of the Book of Common Prayer

The *Book of Common Prayer* is a tertiary authority for the Church of England. This is because it gives liturgical expression to the faith and practice of the Church of England as set out in the *Thirty-Nine Articles*, a pattern of faith and practice which is, as we have seen, in accordance with the Scriptures and the teaching of the Fathers, the Councils of the early church and the catholic creeds.

To put it another way, the *Book of Common Prayer* gives a way of worshipping that is in accordance with Scripture and the witness borne to Scripture by the Fathers. By so doing, it provides a standard for both doctrine (since, as the old maxim goes, *lex orandi lex credendi*, the law of praying is the law of believing) and for further liturgical developments.

Two examples will serve to illustrate this point.

First, the prayer of General Thanksgiving runs as follows:

> Almighty God, Father of all mercies, we thine unworthy servants do give thee most humble and hearty thanks for all thy goodness and loving-kindness to us and to all men; We bless thee for our creation, preservation, and all the blessings of this life; but above all for thine inestimable love in the redemption of the world by our Lord Jesus Christ, for the means of grace, and for the hope of glory. And we beseech thee, give us that due sense of all thy mercies, that our hearts may be unfeignedly thankful, and that we shew forth thy praise, not only with our lips, but in our lives; by giving up ourselves to thy service, and by walking before thee in holiness and righteousness all our days; through Jesus Christ our Lord, to whom with thee and the Holy Ghost be all honour and glory, world without end. Amen.

In terms of doctrine this prayer gives us the big picture of all the actions of God for which we ought to be thankful, and how with God's assistance we should respond to what he has done for us. Liturgically, it offers a model for other prayers of thanksgiving.

Secondly, the alternative prayer after the reception of the elements at Holy Communion runs as follows:

> Almighty and everliving God, we most heartily thank thee, for that thou dost vouchsafe to feed us, who have duly received these holy mysteries, with the spiritual food of the most precious Body and Blood of thy Son our Saviour Jesus Christ; and

dost assure us thereby of thy favour and goodness towards us; and that we are very members incorporate in the mystical body of thy Son, which is the blessed company of all faithful people; and are also heirs through hope of thy everlasting kingdom, by the merits of the most precious death and passion of thy dear Son. And we most humbly beseech thee, O heavenly Father, so to assist us with thy grace, that we may continue in that holy fellowship, and do all such good works as thou hast prepared for us to walk in; through Jesus Christ our Lord, to whom, with thee and the Holy Ghost, be all honour and glory, world without end. Amen.

Doctrinally, this prayer summarises what God does for us when we receive communion and how with God's help we need to respond. Liturgically, it offers a model for other post-communion prayers.

In addition, the Catechism provides those baptised as infants and preparing for confirmation with a concise and reliable guide to the things that they most need to know about the Christian faith. In the words of Frank Colquhoun, 'the value of the Catechism is that it is concise and comprehensive, simple and scriptural. It adheres firmly to the essential facts of the Christian religion and refuses to get side-tracked on secondary issues.'[1]

---

[1] Frank Colquhoun, *The Catechism and the Order of Confirmation* (London: Hodder and Stoughton, 1963), 15.

B. The Ordinal

The development and contents of the Ordinal

The 1549 Prayer Book did not have an ordinal, that is, a set of ordination services. An ordinal was subsequently produced in 1550 and this was revised in 1552 and continued in use after the accession of Elizabeth I. Like the *Book of Common Prayer*, the 1552 *Ordinal* was abolished during the Civil War and the Commonwealth. It was revised in 1662 and remains authorised for in use in the Church of England today as one of the 'historic formularies.'

The full title of the *Ordinal* is 'The form and manner of making ordaining and consecrating of Bishops, Priests and Deacons according to the order of the Church of England'.

Each of these three rites contains the same four basic elements:

- Bible readings which set out the biblical basis for the ministry of deacons, priests or bishops
- a short oral examination of the candidates for ordination designed to show that they understand and accept the responsibilities of the ministry into which they will be ordained
- the act of ordination in which there is prayer and the laying on of hands by a bishop (or bishops in the case of the consecration of a bishop)
- prayers for those ordained and for the church as a whole

The purpose of the Ordinal

There are four reasons why the English Reformers and their seventeenth-century successors produced this particular ordinal.

1. They believed that no one should minister in the church without having received proper authorisation to do so. Having an ordinal was a way of ensuring this principle was observed. It was the way of ensuring that ministers in the Church of England were properly authorised.

2. They intended to perpetuate the traditional threefold order of Bishops, Priests and Deacons. As the Preface to the *Ordinal* makes clear, the English Reformers believed that 'it is evident unto all men diligently reading holy Scripture and ancient Authors, that from the apostles' time there have been these Orders of Ministers in Christ's church; Bishops, Priests and Deacons.' The purpose of the *Ordinal* was to ensure 'that these Orders may be continued, and reverently used and esteemed, in the Church of England.'

3. They intended to ensure continuity of episcopal ordination. The English Reformers believed that episcopal ordination was the historic pattern for the authorisation of ministry that had been handed down from the earliest days of the church and the *Ordinal* was intended to perpetuate it in the Church of England.

4. They intended to produce a biblical ordinal. That is to say, they intended to continue the biblical practice of ordaining people through the laying on of hands (see Acts 6:6, 14:23, 1 Timothy 4:14) in a manner that avoided anything that was 'superstitious and ungodly' (Article XXXVI) and they further intended that the Ordination service

should make clear the biblical pattern of ministry to which those being ordained were called. This was to be done both though the biblical readings chosen for the three rites. It was also to be done through the way in which the prayers, and the questions addressed to the ordinands in their oral examination, reflect biblical language and teaching about the nature of Christian ministry and place reading and preaching the Bible at the heart of ministry.

The authority of the Ordinal

The *Ordinal* has tertiary doctrinal authority for the Church of England for four reasons:

1. The existence of the *Ordinal* points to the biblical and Patristic principle that those who exercise ministry in the church need to be properly authorised to do so. If anyone could minister simply because they felt like doing so, there would be no need for an ordinal.

2. The Preface to the *Ordinal* points to the truth that there is a historic threefold pattern of ministry consisting of the ministry of bishops, priests and deacons that has come down to us from the time of the apostles and that because of its apostolic basis this pattern of ministry needs to be 'continued and reverently esteemed.'

3. The way ordination is conducted in the rites in the *Ordinal* points us to the fact that since the earliest days of the church, the way that ministry has been authorised has been through the laying on of hands with prayer by those with episcopal authority (first the apostles and then the bishops who succeeded them as the senior leaders of the church).

4. The *Ordinal* faithfully reflects the teaching of the Bible about the nature and vital importance of Christian ministry and the responsibilities of those who are called to exercise it.

For further reading

Brian Cummings, *The Book of Common Prayer: A Very Short Introduction* (Oxford: OUP, 2018).

Prudence Dailey (ed.), *The Book of Common Prayer: Past, Present and Future* (London and New York: Continuum, 2011).

Guides to the services in the *Book of Common Prayer* and to the *Ordinal* can be found in the Latimer Trust's Anglican Foundations series (details at https://www.latimertrust.org/product-page/anglican-foundations-series).

Conclusion: Deep Roots Unreached by the Frost

By basing its doctrine not only on the Word of God in Scripture but also on the secondary witness of the Fathers, Councils and creeds of the early church and the tertiary witness of its own historic formularies, the Church of England is saying that if we want to confess the faith in word and deed in our own day, in accordance with the Word of God, we must listen to what those who have gone before us have said on this topic and be willing to learn from them.

Furthermore, as we have noted in the course of this study, there is good reason to listen to those secondary and tertiary theological authorities specified by the Church of England. This is because, in spite of the possibility of error and falsehood to which the church in this world is perpetually subject, God's providential care for his church means that it has also maintained a faithful witness down the centuries to the apostolic faith. It is this faithful witness which we find in these subordinate authorities in addition to the primary authority of Scripture.

These subordinate authorities point us to the Scriptures as our primary, God-given source for understanding the apostolic faith and they point us to what the Scriptures have to say to us about who God is, who we are as human beings, what God has done and will do for us, how we can receive the benefits of what God has done for us, and how we can live rightly before him. They also provide us with Scripturally-based models for the worship of God and remind us about the threefold pattern of ordained ministry instituted by the apostles.

They tell us how the exercise of ordained ministry may rightly be authorised and what the proper exercise of ordained ministry involves.

It is possible that someone might agree with all that has been said about what we can learn from these subordinate authorities, but might still ask why the Church of England points us to subordinate authorities from the past. In his introduction to a translation of Athanasius' book *On the Incarnation of the Word of God,* C. S. Lewis suggests that there are two reasons for giving priority to reading works from the past, what he calls 'old books.'

The first is because we need to study old books to make a right judgement about new ones:

> A new book is still on its trial and the amateur is not in a position to judge it. It has to be tested against the great body of Christian thought down the ages, and all its hidden implications (often unsuspected by the author himself) have to be brought to light.
>
> Often it cannot be fully understood without the knowledge of a good many other modern books. If you join at eleven o'clock a conversation which began at eight you will often not see the real bearing of what is said. Remarks which seem to you very ordinary will produce laughter or irritation and you will not see why – the reason, of course, being that the earlier stages of the conversation have given them a special point.

> In the same way sentences in a modern book which look quite ordinary may be directed at some other book; in this way you may be led to accept what you would have indignantly rejected if you knew its real significance. The only safety is to have a standard of plain, central Christianity ('mere Christianity' as Baxter called it) which puts the controversies of the moment in their proper perspective. Such a standard can be acquired only from the old books.[1]

The second reason Lewis gives to study old books is because only *old* books will challenge the accepted outlook of the present day:

> Every age has its own outlook. It is specially good at seeing certain truths and specially liable to make certain mistakes. We all, therefore, need the books that will correct the characteristic mistakes of our own period. And that means the old books.
>
> All contemporary writers share to some extent the contemporary outlook – even those, like myself, who seem most opposed to it. Nothing strikes me more when I read the controversies of past ages than the fact that both sides were usually assuming without question a good deal which we should now absolutely deny. They thought

---

[1] C. S. Lewis, 'Introduction' in *The Incarnation of the Word of God* (London: Geoffrey Bless, 1944), 6. Extracts reprinted by permission.

> that they were as completely opposed as two sides could be, but in fact they were all the time secretly united – united with each other and against earlier and later ages – by a great mass of common assumptions.
>
> The only palliative is to keep the clean sea breeze of the centuries blowing through our minds, and this can be done only by reading old books. Not, of course, that there is any magic about the past. People were no cleverer then than they are now; they made as many mistakes as we. But not the same mistakes. They will not flatter us in the errors we are already committing; and their own errors, being now open and palpable, will not endanger us. Two heads are better than one, not because either is infallible, but because they are unlikely to go wrong in the same direction. To be sure, the books of the future would be just as good a corrective as the books of the past, but unfortunately we cannot get at them.[2]

For these two reasons given by Lewis, it is important that we should read works from the past to inform our thinking in the present. Of course, not all works from the past are of equal value. There are some which were rightly judged as having little or no value in their own time and which have disappeared into deserved obscurity. However, there are also what we may call classic texts, works that have stood the test of time and have come to be widely recognised as having

---

2   Lewis, *Incarnation of the Word of God*, 6–7.

made a permanent contribution to the development of human thought.

The subordinate authorities to which the Church of England point us come into the latter category. They are classic texts that generation after generation has recognised as permanently contributing to human thought by bearing reliable witness to the apostolic faith in the ways set out above.

The Church of England is therefore right to base its doctrine upon them as well as upon Scripture and to insist that its ministers promise to make use of them 'as your inspiration and guidance under God in bring the grace and truth of Christ to this generation and making Him to those in your care.'

Conversely, the neglect of the study of these classic texts in the contemporary Church of England is a scandal that goes a long way to explain the Church of England's current spiritual weakness. This neglect of 'old books' helps to explain why the church has become increasingly captive to modern secular thought, why it increasingly (mis)reads Scripture in the light of that thought, and why in consequence. it is increasingly unable to act as the salt and light it is called to be (Matthew 5:13–16).

To change this situation, those in the Church of England need to return to the sources of their doctrine. This means studying Scripture above all, but it also means learning to read Scripture with the help provided by those other subordinate doctrinal authorities which the Church of England has traditionally recognised.

To put it another way, in *The Lord of the Rings*, Tolkien writes:

> The old that is strong does not wither,
> Deep roots are not reached by the frost.[3]

Taken together, the doctrinal authorities recognised by the Church of England constitute the old that is strong and does not wither. They are the deep roots of authentic Christian belief and practice that are not reached by the frost of modern secular thought and to which, in consequence, Anglican Christians need constantly to return.

---

3   J. R. R. Tolkien, *The Lord of the Rings* (London: Book Club Associates, 1980), 186.

Also by Martin Davie, in our Anglican Foundation series

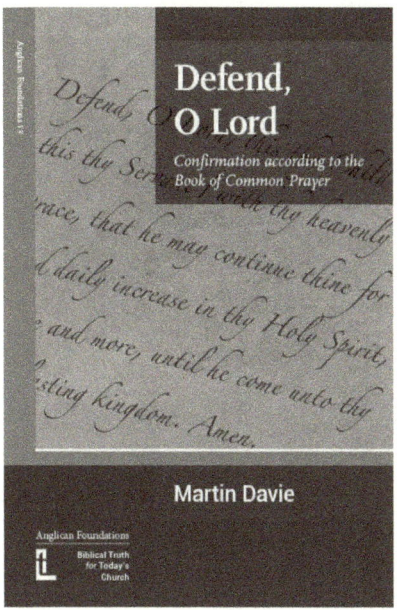

A key way in which the benefits of the work of Christ are conveyed to those who respond to the gospel with repentance and faith is through the two rites of 'Christian initiation': baptism and confirmation. In baptism we die to our old life of sin and death and rise to a new life with God which will be fully revealed at the resurrection of the dead at the end of time.

In confirmation we reaffirm the promises which were made at our baptism, and we are given strength through the Spirit to live the new life we have been given in baptism, and protection from all that would turn us away from God.

The Church of England's normative confirmation service, to which the *Common Worship* services are authorised alternatives, is the confirmation service in the 1662 *Book of Common Prayer*.

This little book provides an introduction to the 1662 service. It describes how confirmation developed in the Early Church and during the Middle Ages and how the Prayer Book confirmation service developed after the Reformation. It also provides a detailed commentary on the Prayer Book service and answers the ten key questions people today generally ask about confirmation.

In our NEW Christian Leadership series

Bishops: A Concise Study summarises the key points of the argument of Martin's major study *Bishops Past, Present and Future* (Gilead Books 2022). It is designed to meet the needs of those who would like to know about the role and importance of bishops in the Church of England, but who would baulk at tackling the 800+ pages of the original book.

This concise study is published in the hope that it will help many in the Church of England, both ordained and lay, to think in a more informed fashion about how bishops should respond to the challenges and opportunities facing the Church of England at this critical point in its history.

Anglican polity has traditionally favoured the incumbent as sole elder over a congregation. Biblical and missional imperatives press for eldership to be plural but how can this be done within an Anglican setting?

This study explores the biblical and historical background to plural eldership or locally shared pastoral leadership. It goes on to describe the experience of nine UK Anglican pastors who have established a team that functions as a plural eldership. While the focus is on the church's ministry of making disciples, lessons are drawn for other areas of pastoral leadership.

The revised and expanded edition includes additional chapters on the role of women and on the place of power in pastoral ministry.

www.ingramcontent.com/pod-product-compliance
Lightning Source LLC
Chambersburg PA
CBHW031458040426
42444CB00007B/1139